Literary Cities of Italy

Also in this series:

Literary Cafés of Paris
  by Noël Riley Fitch

Literary Neighborhoods of New York
  by Marcia Leisner

Literary Villages of London
  by Luree Miller

LITERARY
CITIES
OF
ITALY

William B. Whitman

STARRHILL PRESS
Washington & Philadelphia

For those two wonderful fellow-travelers,
Cammie and Ellis, *con molto amore*

Starrhill Press, publisher
P.O. Box 32342
Washington, D.C. 20007
(202) 686-6703

Illustrations by Jonel Sofian.
Maps by Deb Norman.
Hand-marbled paper by Iris Nevins, Sussex, N.J.

Library of Congress Cataloging-in-Publication Data

Whitman, William B.
    Literary cities of Italy / William B. Whitman.—1st ed.
        p.   cm.
    Includes bibliographical references and index.
    ISBN 0-913515-56-6 (pbk.) : $7.95
    1. Literary landmarks—Italy—Guide-books.   2. Authors—Homes and
  haunts—Italy—Guide-books.   3. Italy—Intellectual life.   4. Italy-
  Description and travel—Guide-books.   I. Title.
PQ4061.W48   1990
809'.8945—dc20   90-38977
                                                                       CIP

Printed in the United States of America.
First edition
9 8 7 6 5 4 3 2 1

Contents

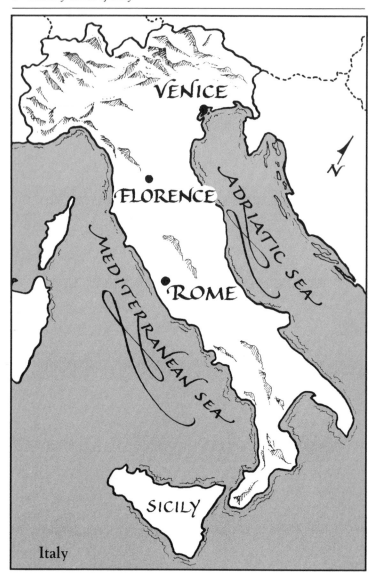

Italy

Rome

MOST OF US, absorbed by the Roman trinity of tombs, temples and *trattorie,* tend to forget that Rome has been a literary mecca for more than 2600 years.

In the days of empire, when it truly was "the city of cities," Rome attracted the best writers and artists of classical times, who came here seeking fame, fortune or a wealthy patron. For centuries after the Fall, another kind of traveler flocked to Rome, drawn by the rise of Christianity, the Papacy and a seemingly inexhaustible supply of venerable places. But in the late 17th century the religious were joined by the creative, and Rome became a "must" on the literary grand tour.

Our tour of Rome's literary landmarks took only one day, which should be seen as a minimum for those who love to meander through and explore historic cities. Time and again we were lured down medieval side streets and cobbled alleys to investigate the street scenes, markets, shops and other delights of Lord Byron's "city of the soul." Your own soul will probably be happier with a more leisurely pace. Even on the second half of our tour, when we left downtown Rome to visit the Protestant Cemetery, we found in this more modern part of town unexpected diversions that could have extended our wanderings by hours or even days. We also discovered that, while the Cemetery and several other places of literary interest are open to the public, most residences are still private apartments just as they were when great writers called them home long ago.

Rome Walk, Part 1: Below the Steps

When in the 18th and 19th centuries Rome became a major target
for literary and artistic travelers, the **Piazza di Spagna (1)** was its
bull's-eye. Visitors from the north arrived on the ancient Via
Flaminia, entered the city through Pope Alexander VII's magnificent front door, the Piazza del Popolo, and then followed the Via
del Babuino a few blocks to the Piazza di Spagna, where most
foreigners found lodging. The area around Via Sistina at the top of
the Spanish Steps, which dominate the piazza, became known to
Romans as "the artists' ghetto," while downstairs, the Piazza di
Spagna, where most of the British "milords" gathered, was labeled
"the English ghetto."

Besides the obvious attractions of a spectacular setting adorned
by Bernini's fountain and the Spanish steps, the piazza had some
eminently practical aspects to recommend it as a place to live. The
narrowness of the surrounding streets made it impossible for the
large traveling coaches of the day to go farther—it was literally
the end of the line. The **Via delle Carrozze (2)** ("street of the
carriages") at the western end of the piazza was where the massive
coaches were repaired after their long journeys. Nevertheless, as
that intrepid 18th-century British traveler and novelist Tobias
Smollett noted, "The Piazza d'Espagna is open, airy and pleasantly
situated. . . . Here most of the English reside." A Smollett
contemporary advised British visitors seeking Italian cooks to write
to "the Inglish Taylor who lives on the Place d'Spain where all the
Inglish lives."

If you stand in the Piazza di Spagna, close your eyes slightly,
and exercise only a little imagination, you can find yourself back in
that long-ago "Place d'Spain." Buildings from Smollett's time still
surround the piazza, the Spanish Embassy that gave the square its
name centuries ago continues to function at No. 56, Bernini's
barcaccia spouts water as it has since 1629, horses and carriages
continue to await foreign travelers, and the Spanish Steps still
display the latest Roman and foreign youth.

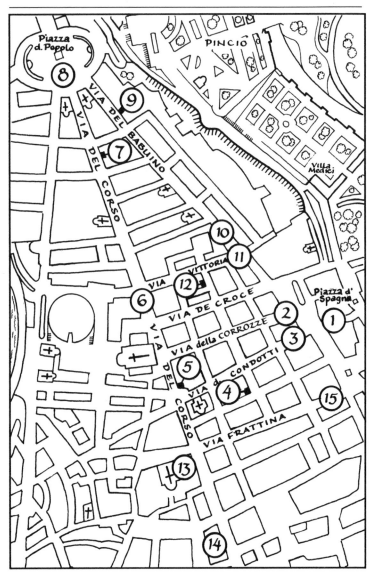

Several important literary landmarks are located in the Piazza di Spagna, including the Keats and Shelley Memorial House at No. 26, next to the Spanish Steps. It is open in summer Monday to Friday 9–1 and 3–6, and in winter 9–1 and 2:30–5:30; closed Saturdays, Sundays and all of August.

In this house John Keats spent three desperate months from November 1820 until his death in February 1821. It is now a fine museum that memorializes not only the English poets John Keats and Percy Bysshe Shelley, but a number of other 19th-century English and American writers, many with Roman connections. The Keats and Shelley exhibits include manuscripts, autograph letters, prints and other memorabilia of the two writers. The museum's dark wood library of more than eight thousand volumes also contains books and mementos of the English poets Lord Byron and Alfred, Lord Tennyson, playwright and novelist Oscar Wilde and essayist William Hazlitt. The room where Keats died overlooks the steps, where the perpetually lively youth scene contrasts poignantly with the tragedy of another young man's struggle for life during a long and dreary Roman winter almost two centuries ago.

We can pay our caloric respects to the grand tour travelers of Smollett's time by visiting Babington's Tea Room, across the steps from the museum at Piazza di Spagna 23. This ancient cafe, with its heavy wooden furniture, fusty decorations and creaky floors, virtually reeks of times past. Babington's dates from the 18th century and has always been an important gathering place for English visitors.

F. Scott and Zelda Fitzgerald spent the winter of 1924 a few doors away at Piazza di Spagna 15, now an office building but then the Hotel Principe, which Scott called "small, unfashionable but most comfortable."

Finally, at Piazza di Spagna 66, Lord Byron took lodging in May 1817 and began work on his epic *Childe Harold*. It was here that he carried out firsthand research for the fourth canto, where he movingly describes classical Rome and its monuments and tombs, including of course the statue *The Dying Gladiator,* which can still be found in room 1 of the Capitoline Museum.

Via Condotti (3), where many famous writers once took lodging, is now the hub of Rome's most elegant shopping district. A few steps from the piazza, at No. 86, is the Caffe Greco where, for more than two centuries, in crowded little rooms with tobacco smoke, many world literary figures gathered and gossiped. The Greco, always one of Europe's leading literary landmarks, was founded in the early 18th century by a transplanted Greek and soon became a favorite rendezvous for foreign residents and visitors. At the Greco you might have found Casanova awaiting one of the assignations described in his memoirs, or perhaps less athletic luminaries such as the great German poet and playwright Johann Wolfgang Goethe, the Russian novelist Nikolai Gogol, the American Mark Twain, or the English Brownings—poets Robert and Elizabeth Barrett.

The Caffe Greco has been beautifully preserved and still looks the way it did in its golden days. Its small rooms are crowded with busts, portraits of famous customers such as Buffalo Bill and paintings donated by former habitués. Although today's clientele runs more to affluent shoppers than to literary giants, marble table tops and perfect service from waiters in swallowtail coats make it easy to visualize a time when this noisy and smoky *caffe* was a focal point for the world's writing talent.

Although many literary visitors practically lived at the Greco, one of the 19th century's best-known and best-loved writers actually did live here. On his 1861 visit Hans Christian Andersen, Danish writer of children's tales, took rooms at the Greco to resume his love affair with "the city of all cities in the world." On an earlier stay in 1834, as an unknown and impoverished youth, Andersen had gathered material and impressions for his first literary success, *The Improvisatore,* an autobiographical novel set in Italy. His 1861 return visit lasted only a month, but he developed a strong friendship with the kingpin of Rome's 19th-century expatriate community, the American writer and sculptor William Wetmore Story. The Story apartment in the Palazzo Barberini (just off the Bernini staircase in the left wing; the space is now occupied by the Gallery of Ancient Art) was the scene of a memorable children's birthday party during which Andersen read "The Ugly Duckling" and Robert Browning narrated "The Pied Piper," after which these two and Story (with flute) led a grand march through the enormous apartment.

Across the street from the Greco, at No. 11, was the inn where Tennyson and the English novelist William Makepeace Thackeray stayed during their Roman visits. Following Via Condotti, turn left on Via Bocca di Leone to visit the **Hotel d'Inghilterra (4)**, at No. 14. Mark Twain stayed here in 1867 when he was writing *Innocents Abroad.* Two years later novelist Henry James (claimed by both the United States, where he was born, and England, where he spent much of his adult life) checked in on his first trip to Rome and at the Inghilterra experienced the ecstatic state that affects many first-time visitors to the city:

> At last—for the first time—I live! It beats everything. It leaves the Rome of your fancy—your education—nowhere. . . . I went reeling and moaning through the streets in a fever of enjoyment.

On the morning of his arrival James raced from the Inghilterra, too thrilled to eat breakfast, and was "promptly rewarded, on the adjacent edge of Via Condotti, by the brightest and strangest [vision] of them all . . . the great rumbling, black-horses coach of the Pope."

Follow James's excited steps to the Via Condotti and then to Via del Corso 126, where the **Hotel Plaza (5)**, then called the Hotel de Rome, hosted James on his 1872 return visit. A few days after checking in, James began work on "From a Roman Notebook," which chronicled his life among Rome's American colony and his explorations of the city and surrounding countryside.

Unlike the Via Condotti, the nearby **Via del Corso (6)**, once one of Rome's most elegant streets, is now given over to jeans, hamburgers, sweat shirts and other detritus of teenage consumption. The Corso is always crowded; even in the last century James observed that it was a "perpetual crush."

Via del Corso 20 was **Goethe's home (7)** during his 1786–88 stay. Although a plaque on the palazzo wall marks the occasion, the best memento of all is *Italian Journey,* Goethe's fascinating and detailed travel diary. His first reaction to Rome's sensuality and vitality was no less ecstatic than that of the buttoned-up Henry James. Just after he arrived Goethe wrote, "At last I have arrived in the first city of the world, [where] one feels exhausted after so much looking and admiring."

The Casa di Goethe is today a museum of photographs, prints, books and other materials related to Goethe's travels in Italy. It also holds Goethe's sketches and manuscripts. The museum's usual hours are 10–1 and 4–5, closed Mondays; unfortunately it is often closed other days as well.

The nearby **Piazza del Popolo (8)** was Rome's great ceremonial gateway for travelers arriving from the north on the Via Flaminia. It still provides a splendid welcome to the city, with a 13th-century B.C. Egyptian obelisk, the Bernini gate dating from 1655 and the 11th-century church of Santa Maria del Popolo, which boasts two Caravaggios and an exquisite Pinturicchio. A number of excellent restaurants and sidewalk cafes can be found in the piazza and its surrounding streets.

The former **Hotel de Russie (9)**, another historic hotel, is located just off the piazza at Via del Babuino 9. The Russie is now the Rome headquarters of RAI, the Italian state radio-TV network, but in the 19th century it saw many distinguished visitors, including Henry James, who stayed here in March 1881.

English novelist Charles Dickens stayed at the Russie during his 1844 visit to Rome. His wanderings and highly subjective opinions about the city, its art and its people were later included in *Pictures from Italy*, a travel masterpiece in which Dickens makes Rome as vivid as the London of his novels.

Dickens arrived on a cold and blustery day in January 1844, just in time for the last two days of Carnival, when celebrations were at their wildest. In those days the Corso was the center of all Carnival activity, with horse races down to the Piazza Venezia and elaborately costumed Romans pelting each other with confetti and cakes. On the last night of Carnival, Dickens observed a rowdy contest, now long vanished, in which thousands of celebrants attempt by all available means to extinguish each others' candles, or *moccoli*.

After the last *moccolo* went out Dickens began "conscientiously to work, to see Rome . . . making acquaintance with every post and pillar in the city." This was no exaggeration. Dickens saw it all, including a public execution near the church of San Giovanni Decollato and the equally gory paintings of early martyrdoms in the church of Santo Stefano Rotondo, which can still horrify. He visited the Vatican often, taking in religious spectacles like the papal footwashing, complete with a reenactment of the Last

The Tiber River

Supper, and the Vatican Museums, which gave him opportunities to hold forth on Bernini ("the most detestable class of productions in the wide world") and most of Rome's other sculptures ("intolerable abortions"). Despite these dubious judgments, Dickens, like his intellectual predecessor, Juvenal, remains one of our best interpreters of what has always been and will doubtless remain a teeming, tumultuous and disorderly city.

Moving past the expensive antique shops and art galleries of **Via del Babuino (10)**, we enter the Rome of the Brownings by turning right on the **Via Vittoria (11)**. On the corner at the Via Bocca di Leone stood the home of "the wretched Comparini" and their daughter Pompilia, whose lives and deaths in a triple homicide Robert Browning immortalized in the epic *The Ring and the Book.* The Brownings had lived nearby in 1853, at **Via Bocca di Leone 43 (12)**; you can stop for a snack at the lively neighborhood fruit and vegetable market just in front of their house.

Pompilia was married and buried just a short walk from here, at the church of **San Lorenzo in Lucina (13)** (Lorenzo's church) which you reach by proceeding past Via Condotti to Via Frattina and turning right into the piazza just past the Corso. San Lorenzo, which dates from A.D. 366, is of immense interest for the giant sundial of the Emperor Augustus and the Roman houses that lie beneath the church (underground tours every Saturday at 11 A.M.). Browning readers will immediately recognize the 12th-century stone lions in the church portico as the fierce marble creatures of Pompilia's childhood "eating the figure of a prostrate man / (to the right, it is, of entry by the door)."

Returning to the Corso and turning right we soon arrive at No. 374, now the headquarters of a large Italian bank, Credito Italiano, but once the **Palazzo Verospi (14)**. A plaque on the building opposite the Rinascente department store reminds visitors that this was Shelley's home in the spring of 1819. Shelley was accompanied by his wife Mary, his son William, or "Willmouse," and Claire Clairmont, Byron's former mistress (and Mary's stepsister). Shelley and his family spent their days enjoying the Roman museums and driving among the fountains and statues in the Villa Borghese. But "in the purple and golden light of an Italian evening" Shelley often went out alone to walk in the "sublime desolation" of the Roman Forum. Mornings would often find him in the Baths of Caracalla sketching and writing *Prometheus Unbound,* which he largely completed that spring. He also completed *The Cenci* during this period.

Shelley's Roman spring ended in tragedy, with the death of his four-year-old son. Little Willmouse was buried in Rome's Protestant Cemetery, not far from the spot where his father's ashes were interred only a few years later.

We retrace our steps back down the Via del Corso to **Via Frattina (15)**, another important shopping street.

On July 31, 1906, the 24-year-old Irish expatriate writer James Joyce, accompanied by Nora Barnacle and their infant son, Giorgio, arrived in Rome from Trieste. Joyce had been working in Trieste as a language teacher at Berlitz but was lured to Rome by the prospect of better pay as the English-speaking correspondent at a Rome bank, a job he hoped would allow more time for writing. The Joyces settled in immediately at Via Frattina 52, in a second-floor apartment owned by a Madame Dufour. In this building Joyce began work on *Ulysses* and completed *The Dubliners.* Nevertheless, his stay in Rome proved disastrous. His job in the bank (the building still stands at Via San Claudio 87, corner of Via del Corso) consumed time Joyce had hoped to spend writing, and financial difficulties compelled him to moonlight as a teacher in a local language school. Evidently even this did not suffice, for Madame Dufour evicted the Joyce family and they spent their final days in Rome in dingy rooms by the Tiber (Via Monte Brianzo 51). As a final blow, Joyce had an experience that befalls many foreign visitors—after spending the evening in an *osteria,* he was robbed of his final paycheck. Two days later the Joyces retreated to Trieste.

Follow Via Frattina back to the Piazza di Spagna. As you climb the Spanish Steps, keep in mind Dickens's description of the steps in the last century, when they were frequented by artists' models seeking work: "There is [a] man in a blue cloak who always pretends to be asleep in the sun and who, I need not say, is always very wide awake and very attentive to the disposition of his legs. This is the *dolce far niente* model. There is another man in a brown cloak, who leans against the wall, with his arms folded in his mantle, and looks out of the corners of his eyes, which are just visible beneath his broad slouched hat. This is the assassin model."

The Spanish Steps

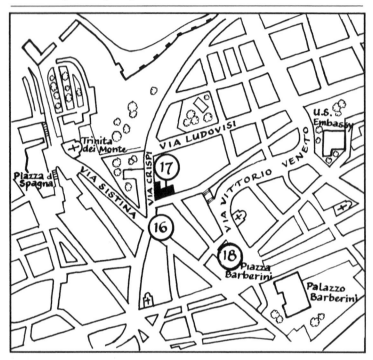

Rome Walk, Part 2: Above the Steps

Via Sistina 125 (16) was the home of Nikolai Gogol from 1837 to 1840. This escapee from the gloom of 19th-century Russia underwent a spectacular transformation during his years in the Italian sun. Gogol adored Rome and was a joyful and practically insatiable visitor, covering the city in vast touristic swoops and gulps, effusing and sketching all the way, even on the table tops at the Caffe Greco. The euphoria he felt in Rome induced him to date his letters to Moscow from the year of Rome's founding: 1838, for him, became 2588. Gogol's voracious habits extended to the table. His gluttony in favorite *trattorie*, such as Falcone's, near the Pantheon at Via Monterone 83, and Lepre's, on Via Condotti across from the Caffe Greco, is well documented. But fortunately the pen is mightier than the fork; Gogol's literary achievements while in Rome are far more memorable than his bouts of gluttony. Standing at his desk in the Via Sistina apartment, Gogol dictated much of his most famous work, *Dead Souls.*

The Via Francesco Crispi, which runs steeply uphill from the Via Sistina, was in classical times the Via Salaria Vetus, the urban stretch of the great consular road connecting Rome with the port of Brindisi and the Middle East. During the first half of 1858 it was home to American novelist Nathaniel Hawthorne, his wife and two daughters, who lived in the elegant **Palazzo Sarazani (17)** at Via Crispi 90, a few doors uphill from the corner of Via degli Artisti. A wrought iron "S" still crowns the doorway. Hawthorne had just completed an assignment as the American Consul in Liverpool and was already well established, thanks to *The House of Seven Gables* and *The Scarlet Letter.*

Hawthorne's fascinating *Notebooks,* which include some of the finest travel writing of the period, recount an astonishing number of visits to Rome's classical sites, trips in the countryside and a hyperactive social life within Rome's American community. They also show Hawthorne to be a thoughtful and sometimes amusing observer of places and people, particularly of the foibles of Americans. Who among us, for example, has not experienced "that peculiar lassitude and despondency . . . which has so often afflicted me while viewing works of art."

In Rome Hawthorne began to sketch out *The Marble Faun,* an allegorical novel that drew upon his Roman experiences and sensory recollections. The title comes from Praxiteles' noted statue, *Satyr Resting,* which can be found in room 1 on the first floor of the Capitoline Museum, exactly where Hawthorne himself came upon it in April 1858.

From Via Crispi, walk down Via Sistina, a street with numerous snack bars, to the subway stop at **Piazza Barberini (18)**.

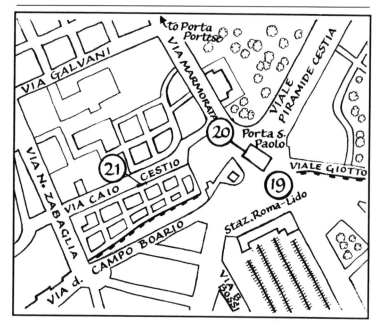

Rome Walk, Part 3: The Protestant Cemetery

Catch a train to the **Piramide subway station (19).** You will
surface at the **Porta San Paolo (20),** where, in the year 62, St.
Paul left Rome on the way to martyrdom. The same stones of the
Via Ostiensis that Paul trod that final day are still here under the
ancient gate, and the Pyramid of Caius Cestius, which Paul surely
saw on his final journey, still stands gleaming and white as it did
when Paul passed by almost two thousand years ago.

Behind the pyramid and between the massive walls that the
Emperor Honorarius built several centuries later lies one of Rome's
most peaceful and tranquil areas, the **Protestant Cemetery (21).**
With its dark green cypresses and pines, the cemetery is the final
resting place of hundreds of non-Catholic foreigners who, willingly
or not, stayed on in Rome forever. The cemetery entrance is at Via

Caio Cestio 6; it is open all day, but visitors must ring for admission.

Most Anglo-Americans head immediately for the graves of Keats and Shelley. Keats' gravestone, in the newer part of the cemetery, does not bear his name, but simply the epitaph, "Here lies one whose name was writ in water." He is prominently mentioned, however, on the adjoining stone of his friend Joseph Severn.

Further along the same path, against the ancient town wall, is another pair of graves—those of Percy Bysshe Shelley and fellow poet Edward Trelawney. "*Cor Cordium*" (heart of all hearts) is the inscription on Shelley's grave, but his heart is not buried with him here in Rome. After the poet drowned near Viareggio and was cremated on the beach by Byron and Trelawney, his heart was returned to England. Only his ashes stayed on in Italy.

A few steps from Shelley's grave stands *The Angel of Grief,* which marks the tomb of William Wetmore Story and his wife. "W. W." Story, the son of a prominent Boston jurist, came to Rome in 1846 and stayed on until his death in 1895. He was a friend to almost every notable visitor. The dazzling Story family entertained and befriended the Brownings, Nathaniel Hawthorne, American writer and teacher James Russell Lowell, Hans Christian Andersen and many others. Few Americans today are familiar with the accomplishments of this writer and sculptor whose charm, intelligence and warmth inspired Henry James to write *William Wetmore Story and his Friends,* an affectionate biography.

A visit to the cemetery can easily be combined with a visit to the Sunday morning flea market at Porta Portese only a few blocks away. One of Europe's longest, cheapest and most touristic streetcar lines, the No. 30 tram, stops within a few feet of both the cemetery and the market.

The Uffizi, the Palazzo Vecchio and the Duomo

Florence

MENTION FLORENCE to most Americans and you conjure up visions of the Uffizi and its magnificent collection of paintings and sculpture, or of the Pitti Palace with its sublime Raffaellos, Titians and Rubens—two temples of art that for centuries have made this medium-sized city one of the world's great cultural centers. Everyone also associates Florence with the truly universal man, Leonardo da Vinci, and those other princes of Italian art, Raffaello and Michelangelo. More recently, Florence has come to be thought of also as the global center of another art—the design and manufacture of shoes, clothing and textiles, not to mention the superb leather goods that are available on practically every corner. No matter what their focus, visitors also revere Florence's gastronomic past, which gave France its cuisine, and present, which displays astonishing excellence and innovation. But few non-Italians remember that Florence, aside from its glorious achievements in art, fashion and food, was also Italy's preeminent literary center and the home of the Italian language itself.

Here Dante Alighieri, in the late 13th century, wrote *The Divine Comedy,* which helped establish what was then the Tuscan dialect as standard Italian. To this day, well-educated Italian school children are subjected to the tedious task of memorizing entire stanzas of this epic. There are deferred benefits in this, however, for in later life the ability to reel off huge chunks of Dante from memory becomes an impressive cultural and social credential for many Italians. Also in Dante's time, the great humanist poet Petrarch and his close friend Boccaccio, whose tales in *The Decameron* describe Florentine life in the early 14th century, maintained a brilliant literary tradition that was carried forward into the next two centuries by Machiavelli, Vasari and others.

In a rare spurt of enthusiasm, the usually restrained Karl Baedeker, 19th-century father of modern travel guides, told his readers that Florence is "one of the most interesting and attractive places in the world." Possibly under the influence of some early local boosters or the Chamber of Commerce, Baedeker goes on to report that "the Florentines have ever been noted for the vigour of their reasoning powers and for their pre-eminence in artistic talent. . . . Their superiority over the Genoese and other towns of Lombardy is apparent in their manners and dress."

Baedeker was a little late in reporting the excellence of Florentine art and thought; five hundred years earlier, the first English-speaking writer had already visited Florence. Geoffrey Chaucer came here in 1373, attracted by the city's already great literary fame and the opportunity to meet with Boccaccio and other noted Florentine writers of the day. Following Chaucer's early lead, many 18th- and 19th-century writers made Florence a centerpiece of their literary pilgrimages to centers of European literature and culture. The list included many Americans, ranging in personal and literary style from Mark Twain to Henry James and Sinclair Lewis.

But it was mainly the British who flocked to Florence, attracted by the incomparable art and literary tradition, not to mention a cost of living that made Florence a great bargain for foreigners. Life as an expatriate in Florence was more comfortable and certainly cheaper than any lifestyle London could offer, and the climate was vastly better. The large resident British community became quite insular. Social contact with ordinary Italians was for most very limited; even one's shopping was done in expatriate-oriented stores such as Seeber's bookstore on Via Tornabuoni or the Anglo-

American stores on Via Cavour. Ailing foreigners could seek advice in English from Dr. Wilson, also on Via Tornabuoni, or perhaps in the nearby offices of Dr. Henderson; later they could fill their prescriptions at pharmacies in the same neighborhood owned by Dr. Roberts or Dr. Groves. More serious kinds of comfort were available at the eight churches where English was the principal language. There were English schools and several English-language newspapers. Small wonder that Shelley called Florence the "paradise of exiles."

Henry James once expressed delight in the "visitable past"—those places where it is possible to reach out and find the past "firm and continuous." Nowhere is the past more visitable than in Florence, with its profound literary tradition spanning more than six hundred years. The wars and other upheavals that in this century have destroyed much of our continuity with the past have largely spared this timeless city. Our ability to participate in Florence's glorious past remains largely unchanged from the days when James and other great writers made their own excursions of the imagination here.

Florence Walk, Part 1: The Historic Center

While it is possible to make this walk through historic and literary
Florence in one day, it would require a will of iron. Many would
prefer to allow two days, while for some two years is insufficient.

To begin at the beginning, our visit to literary Florence should
start at **Via Santa Margherita 1 (1)**, generally (but not universally)
thought to be where Dante was born and lived until his exile from
the city. The towerlike house, surrounded by a maze of narrow and
picturesque medieval streets, has been much restored since the
time when one of world literature's greatest figures lived here.
Nevertheless, its heavy stone construction and fortified appearance
still convey a strong sense of the world of urban warlords and their
fortress-homes that dominated Florentine life during the violent
days of the 13th century.

In 1302 an ungrateful Florence exiled its greatest poet, but
Dante has his revenge in *The Divine Comedy*, written in exile,
where he calls the Florentines an "ungrateful, malicious lot . . .
miserly, jealous and proud." Dante never returned to Florence; he
died in exile and is buried in Ravenna.

Dante's home is now a museum with displays and exhibits about
his work and times. It is open 9:30–12:30 and 3:30–6:30;
9:30–12:30 only on Sundays and holidays; closed on Wednesdays.

Dante's church, **Santa Margherita de' Cerchi (2)**, is a tiny
12th-century jewel tucked away a few paces from his door on the
narrow street of the same name. Dante married Gemma Donati in
Santa Margherita; her family coat of arms is just above the
entrance.

A right turn after exiting the church leads to the **Via del
Corso 4 (3)**, home of the Beatrice of Dante's poetry—Beatrice
Portinari—"whose image . . . stayed constantly with me." This
lifelong but unattainable love of Dante's was buried in Santa
Margherita; a plaque on Via del Corso with a quote from the
Purgatorio marks her home.

A right turn onto Via dei Calzaioli leads to the imposing

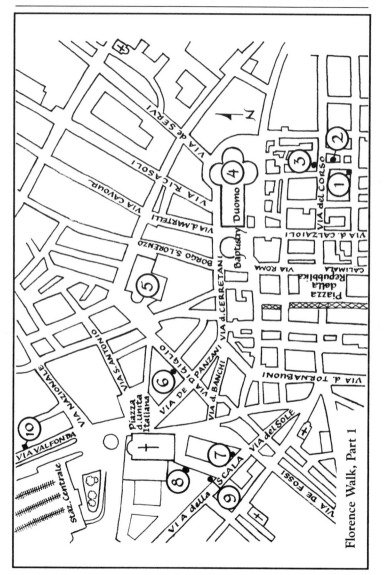

Florence Walk, Part 1

Cathedral (4), or *Duomo,* and the Baptistery of San Giovanni opposite. Henry James remarked on the Duomo's "big bleak interior . . . one of the loveliest works of man's hands." Its single most notable feature is not its gigantic size, although it dwarfs the surrounding streets and buildings, or its imposing interior, but its majestic Brunelleschi dome, a work of 15th-century engineering genius that dominates the city and surroundings. The Baptistery of San Giovanni has evoked awe and admiration over the centuries beginning with Dante, who saluted, "my beautiful San Giovanni" in the *Inferno,* and continuing down to Karl Baedeker, who told his readers that its 14th- and 15th-century gilded bronze doors are "simply perfect . . . a marvel of art."

Borgo San Lorenzo leads from the Baptistery to the church of **San Lorenzo (5)**, the Medici church, which dates from 1426 and contains treasures by Filippo Lippi, Donatello and Brunelleschi. San Lorenzo is best known, however, for its exquisite Medici tombs, which are reached by an outside entrance on Piazza Madonna degli Aldobrandini.

Poems have been written about the tomb of Lorenzo, Duke of Urbino, with Michelangelo's statue of the warrior representing Lorenzo brooding over the carved sarcophagus with figures depicting Dawn and Dusk. Perhaps the finest description of Lorenzo came from a visiting American, Nathaniel Hawthorne, who wrote in 1858,

> It is the one work worthy of Michael Angelo's reputation, and grand enough to vindicate for him all the genius that the world gave him credit for. . . . After looking at it for a while . . . it comes to life. It is as much a miracle to have achieved this as to make a statue that would rise up and walk.

The Medici tombs are open from 9–2 (9–1 on Sundays and holidays) but closed on Mondays.

San Lorenzo's massive dome presides over a sprawling and lively open-air street market with hundreds of stands selling clothing, jewelry and leather goods. The market functions all day every day but is best visited in the morning. Because shopping in Italy is so good for the appetite, the area's main street, Borgo San Lorenzo, is packed with restaurants and *pizzerie.*

In 1638 and 1639, English poet John Milton found lodging in the **Palazzo dei Gaddi (6)**, at Via del Giglio 11, where a plaque commemorates his visit. In later years Milton wrote lovingly of Florence and the close friends he made during his two-month stay. During this time Milton probably met with Galileo, then under a form of house arrest instigated by the Inquisition.

At the end of the Via del Giglio, the Via dei Banchi leads to **Piazza Santa Maria Novella (7)**, which is dominated by the elegant green and white marble facade of its 13th-century church. The Strozzi Chapel, in the south transept, is where Boccaccio's young Florentines gathered in the plague year of 1348 to begin the adventures described in *The Decameron.*

A plaque marking American poet Henry Wadsworth Longfellow's stay at Piazza Santa Maria Novella 16, the **Hotel Minerva (8)**, tells us that this graceful piazza, surrounded by Renaissance houses, some with their original *graffito* facades, was once known as "The Mecca of Foreigners." This is no exaggeration, for in the last century the piazza and its neighborhood was the Florentine base of Henry James and his friend William Dean Howells and of Shelley and Longfellow.

Much earlier however, in 1584, French essayist Michel de Montaigne wrote of watching carriage races in this "large and beautiful piazza." According to Montaigne, a race was held annually on the day of San Giovanni. It involved three circuits around stone obelisks placed at the ends of the piazza. Montaigne noted that these contests were a major civic occasion, often attended by the cream of Florentine nobility, including the Grand Duke of Tuscany, whose carriage won in 1584.

This tradition evidently was long-lived. American novelist James Fenimore Cooper wrote of seeing the same races during his 1828 visit. Although he found the carriages ponderous and clumsy,

Cooper thought the cumulative effect of the elaborate ceremonies and Florentine elegance "quite imposing."

The two stone obelisks used for centuries to delineate the track are still standing in the piazza; for inexplicable reasons they are supported at each corner by a turtle.

In early 1828 Longfellow stayed at a *pensione* that has since been incorporated into the Hotel Minerva. The New England professor was, at age 20, already an expert on early Italian literature and had gone to Florence to study Dante and translate *The Divine Comedy* into English, the first American to do so. Longfellow was also a great admirer of Boccaccio, whose work he later singled out in his own poem, *Tales of a Wayside Inn*, as "joyous Tuscan tales that make Fiesole's green hills and vales remembered for Boccaccio's sake."

Essayist and novelist William Dean Howells, who served as the American Consul in Venice during the Civil War, often stayed at the Minerva on visits to research Dante. But in 1882 he came back to write "Florentine Mosaic," the centerpiece of his collection, *Tuscan Cities*. Howells returned to the Minerva often before his death in 1920. His charming book *Indian Summer* and short stories "The Ragged Lady" and "The Landlord of Lion's Head" all have Florentine settings.

Another noted guest was American essayist and poet Ralph Waldo Emerson, who in April 1838 came to Florence and the Minerva when he was recuperating from tuberculosis and grieving the untimely death of his wife. Emerson explored the beauty of the city, the glories of Santa Croce and the "elegant curve of the Ponte Santa Trinita."

The tall, cream-colored building at the corner of the piazza and Via della Scala was the home of Henry James in 1874, on the first of many visits to Florence. In his "high, charming, shabby old room" at **Via della Scala 2 (9)**, James worked on his first successful novel, *Roderick Hudson*, the tale of an American sculptor in Rome and his unattainable love, Christina Light, the future Princess Cassamassima. On this visit James also finished a travel essay, "The Autumn in Florence," which later formed part of *Italian Hours*.

Not far from the piazza, a plaque at Via Valfonda 2, across from the main railway station, marks the former site of the **Palazzo Marini (10)**, where Percy Bysshe Shelley stayed from October 1819 to January 1820. Although the time that Shelley, his wife Mary and Claire Clairmont spent in Florence was relatively brief, these months saw Shelley, in an explosive burst of creativity, complete three of his finest works, *Prometheus Unbound, Ode to the West Wind* and *Peter Bell the Third*.

During this productive period Shelley also found time to visit the Uffizi every day and write "Notes on Sculptures in Florence," in which he praised his favorite statue, *Venus Anodyomene* ("Crouching Venus" in the South Corridor overlooking the Arno) and complained of others, "Curse these fig leaves; why is a round tin thing more decent than a cylindrical marble one?"

The Shelley entourage left "the most beautiful city in the world" for Pisa during the harsh winter of 1820 in hopes that the move might improve Shelley's poor health. But Pisa was merely another stop on the way to Viareggio, where Shelley, still ailing, drowned just a few years later.

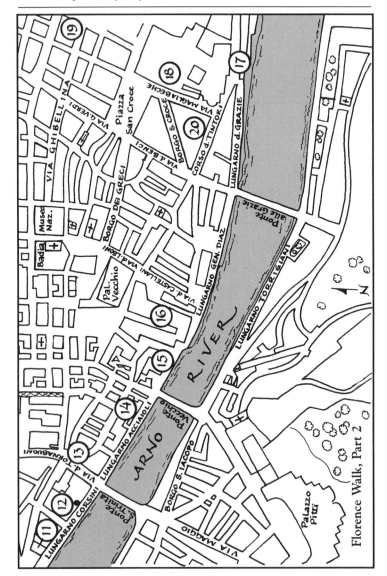

Florence Walk, Part 2

Florence Walk, Part 2: Along the Arno

One of Florence's best streets for antique shopping, the Via de' Fossi, runs from the loggia end of the Piazza Santa Maria Novella to the Arno and the Piazza Goldoni. On the left, at Piazza Goldoni 2, stands the **Palazzo Ricasoli (11)**, with the family crest over the stone doorway. In October 1828, the already well-known American writer (and American Consul in Lyons from 1826–1829) James Fenimore Cooper moved into this palazzo with his large family, taking a ten-room apartment on the first floor just to the left of the entrance.

The chronicler of the Mohicans, creator of Natty Bumppo and interpreter of backwoods America adored the art, sophistication and elegance of Florence, reporting back to friends that "the wine of our palace is among the best of Tuscany. . . . We burn in our lamps oil that you would be happy to get on your lobsters and salads." Cooper also reported with ill-concealed pleasure his presentation at the court of Archduke Leopold II, then located in the Pitti Palace. Unfortunately His Highness had not yet read *The Last of the Mohicans,* and Cooper recounted his patriotic pride in correcting the archduke's serious misconceptions about the geography, history and inhabitants of his exotic homeland. While at Palazzo Ricasoli, Cooper wrote *The Wept of Wish-ton-Wish,* a little-remembered novel that was published in Florence. The archduke's copy can be found today in the *Biblioteca Nazionale,* next to Santa Croce.

Another American resident of Palazzo Ricasoli was poet and editor William Cullen Bryant, who stayed here in late 1835 on the first of five visits. Bryant loved the art, sculpture and tradition of Florence, but he had a special feel for the pageant of everyday Florentine street life, so different from that of his native New England. In his diary he described the changing view from his window over the Arno in the course of a typical day. Before dawn Bryant watched quaintly clad peasants crossing the Ponte alla Carraja to bring their produce to the city markets. Then came the tradesmen, including "bakers boys with a dozen loaves . . . balanced on their heads," followed by maidservants, milkmen and priests. Finally Bryant records in his street scene the zenith of the day, that great moment when "the English, in white hats and white pantaloons, come out of their lodgings, accompanied sometimes by their hale and square-built spouses, and saunter stiffly along the Arno."

Although Baedeker informed his faithful that "the Lungarno is almost deserted in summer on account of the exhalations and mosquitoes which infest it," the boulevard these days is rarely quiet. Although still a street where foreign visitors saunter, it is also a torrent of autos and scooters that flows more quickly than the adjacent river. This riverside avenue is lined with elegant and historic palaces, many of which now house some of Florence's finest (and most expensive) boutiques and antique shops.

The British Consulate, located in **Palazzo Masetti (12)** at Lungarno Corsini 2, was from 1793 to 1824 the home of the Countess of Albany, who presided here over a high-powered literary salon that included Shelley along with French novelists Alexander Dumas, *père,* and Stendhal.

Just after the consulate we enter the Via de' Tornabuoni, one of Italy's great shopping streets, with art galleries, jewelry stores and internationally known shops offering shoes, leather goods and designer clothing, all priced in mega-lire.

Soon after leaving the Lungarno, Via de' Tornabuoni crosses the tiny **Piazza Santa Trinita (13)** and its column dedicated to Cosimo Medici. At No. 11, the massive 13th-century Palazzo Spini-Ferroni once contained the Hotel d'Europe, in its day one of Florence's best hotels. In 1867 the Europe hosted Mark Twain, who was passing through on the famous trip to the Holy Land later described in *Innocents Abroad.* Twain's description of Florence is grumpy and his experiences were "chiefly unpleasant," as is clearly brought home in *Innocents Abroad,* where he rails against Florence's greedy artisans ("They will counterfeit a fly or a high

toned bug or the ruined Coliseum") and artists ("We went to the
Church of Santa Croce . . . to weep over the tombs of
Michelangelo, Raphael and Machiavelli. I suppose they are buried
there, but it may be that they reside elsewhere and rent their tombs
to other parties—such being the fashion in Italy"). Twain also got
lost in "a labyrinth of narrow streets" late one night, finding the
Europe only after an unpleasant run-in with a military patrol.

Twain's next three visits to Florence were much more agreeable.
He returned in 1878 on a walking tour of Europe and again in
1892–93, when he rented the majestic Villa Viviani near
Settignano. The view from the Villa to him was "the fairest picture
on our planet." Twain came back to Settignano in 1903, staying at
the Villa di Quarto, where he wrote *Tom Sawyer Abroad.*

In early 1856 James Russell Lowell also stayed at the Europe
while preparing a Harvard lecture series on Dante. On a longer
visit in 1873–74, Lowell again stayed in Piazza Santa Trinita, but
this time at the Hotel du Nord, just across the way. The Nord was
located at Piazza Santa Trinita 1, in Palazzo Bartolini- Salimbeni,
an aristocratic 16th-century building with a handsome light-colored
stone facade with niches ready for statues that never arrived. It was
also Herman Melville's hotel in 1857.

For most of the 19th century, Piazza Santa Trinita 2 housed one
of literary Florence's main gathering places, the *Gabinetto Scien-
tifico e Literario di G. P. Vieusseux.* A plaque over the door marks
the location. A guidebook of the period tells us that Vieusseux's
was founded in 1826 and was "without doubt, the largest
circulating library in Europe." More than that, Vieusseux's was also
a combination social club for visiting writers and reading room
where regular foreign visitors such as Russian writer Dostoevsky,
Henry James and English statesman-writer Thomas Babington
Macaulay could catch up on happenings back home from
Vieusseux's supply of foreign newspapers. Another habitué, William
Dean Howells, in fact used Vieusseux's as the scene of a major
episode in his novel, *Indian Summer.*

In 1860, after the success of *The Mill on the Floss*, George Eliot and her companion, writer George Henry Lewes, decided that an Italian vacation was in order, especially since the informality of their relationship had already caused considerable commotion and indignation in England. Eliot and Lewes took up lodging at the Pensione Svizzera, located at Via Tornabuoni 13, "the quietest hotel in Florence, having sought it out for the sake of getting clear of the stream of English and Americans." Via Tornabuoni 13 is still a hotel, and one where evidently very little has changed over the intervening years.

While at the Svizzera, Eliot learned of the success of *Silas Marner* and, in October 1861, began work on *Romola*, a historical romance set in Florence. Although it would be wonderful to report that Eliot's tribute to a city she loved has been enduringly successful, in truth *Romola* is today generally ranked as a forgettable effort. Even a contemporary, William Dean Howells, complained that "the author does burden her drama and dialogue with too much history."

The Pensione Svizzera was also the Florence home of Dostoevsky, who stayed here in 1862.

After a trip to Bologna, Eliot and Lewes returned to Florence but this time, possibly because the English and Americans had inundated the Svizzera, moved in at the Hotel Vittoria, at Lungarno Amerigo Vespucci 44.

Return to the Arno, and turn left on the Lungarno Acciaioli. For many years the **Hotel Grande Bretagne (14)**, at Lungarno Acciaioli 8, was one of Florence's top hotels and the favorite of visiting writers successful enough to afford its rates. The site has a history of literary associations going back to the 18th century when, before the hotel was built, the British Embassy reportedly stood here. Here His Majesty's Minister, Sir Horace Mann, had as guests his good friends historian and novelist Horace Walpole and poet Thomas Gray during their 1739–40 visit. Gray wrote that, from his "charming" apartment, the Ponte di Trinita was "the resort of everybody, where they hear music, eat iced fruits and sup by moonlight." Aside from being the British Minister, a well known essayist and, according to Walpole, "the best of creatures," Mann, in his letters to Walpole, gave an excellent portrayal of Florentine life, mores and manners over the many years he lived here.

The hotel, built in 1811, also hosted Stendhal, author of *The Red and the Black,* who returned many times. On one of these trips, Stendhal wrote an early travel guide to Florence entitled *Travel in Italy 1828,* which collected much useful data for the foreign visitor, including where to stay ("at Signora Imbert's") and eat ("the White Lion on Via Vigna Nuova"). Stendhal cautioned that, while you also can eat well at Signora Imbert's, the price is high and "one meets many English." Stendhal thoroughly explored Florence but reserved his highest praise ("Anything I could say would be inadequate") for the Volterrano frescoes in the Niccolini chapel in the north transept of Santa Croce.

Henry James, after finishing *Washington Square* in Paris, checked in at the Grande Bretagne during the spring of 1880 for a two-month stay "in a room with a window on the river yellow in the spring sun." Here he began work on *The Portrait of a Lady,* which is partially set in Florence. In *Italian Hours* James described the view from his window:

> My room at the inn looked out on the river, and was flooded all day with sunshine. There was an absurd orange-colored paper on the walls; the Arno, of a hue not altogether different, flowed beneath; and on the other side of it rose a line of sallow houses, of extreme antiquity, crumbling and mouldering, bulging and protruding over the stream. All this brightness and yellowness was a perpetual delight, . . . a delightful composition.

Although the facade of the Grande Bretagne was destroyed during World War II, some of those houses of extreme antiquity that enchanted James can be seen across the river, still protruding over the Arno just under the bell tower of San Iacopo.

Longfellow also made the Grande Bretagne his headquarters in
1869. "We had a beautiful apartment close by the Ponte Vecchio,
and right in the heart of the medieval town. Close by too was the
little church of Santo Stefano, where Boccaccio read his comment
on Dante." It was in this obviously happy setting that Longfellow
conceived his sonnet about the Ponte Vecchio. Although his
poems have long been part of the American literary fabric, few are
aware of Longfellow's role as one of our earliest Italian scholars and
a leading interpreter of Italian culture to the young republic.

In 1844 another noted guest, Charles Dickens, wrote eloquently
of the city in his *Pictures from Italy* ("Magnificently stern and
sombre are the streets of beautiful Florence"). But Dickens, with
his unerring eye for the human condition, also found time to note
some not-so-beautiful features of Florence, including the local
prison next to the Palazzo Vecchio—"a foul and dismal place . . .
[where] all are squalid, dirty and vile to look at." Just as in
London, Dickens found trouble in this Tuscan Paradise, where he
watched an 80-year-old prisoner being booked and jailed for
murdering a young girl "in the market place full of bright flowers."

Back in the last century Karl Baedeker, writing from the
Teutonic gloom of Leipzig, advised his readers that, in deciding on
a *pensione* in Florence, "it is important to secure rooms with a
southern aspect, which is essential to health and comfort in Italy."
Warming to the subject, he warned his faithful that "the quarter of
the town on the left bank of the Arno, especially below the Porta
San Frediano, is considered less healthy."

The selection of a *pensione* was so important to turn-of-the-
century travelers that the merits and shortcomings of these
boarding houses were hotly and endlessly debated by foreign visitors
and expatriates. Aside from the quality of the table and the
comfort of the room, nationality was also important in choosing
just the right one, for many *pensioni* specialized by nationality.
For example, the Chapman was cited by Baedeker as "frequented
by Americans," while Mme. Jenny Giachino's establishment

apparently concentrated on English visitors, and the Lelli had "chiefly English and American guests."

The most famous Florentine *pensione* of all, however, is the Bertolini of English novelist E. M. Forster's *Room with a View,* that wonderful and satirical account of British visitors to Florence early in this century. Inspired by the success of the book and then the film, a number of Florentine *pensioni* claim to be Forster's model for the Bertolini. Although Forster's mythical *pensione* may have been a composite, most believe that the real Bertolini was in fact the **Quisisana-Pontevecchio (15)**, where the film was shot, on the third floor of Lungarno Archibusieri 4, just past the end of the *Ponte Vecchio.* In the Quisisana's room with a view, No. 15, it is "pleasant to fling wide the windows, . . . to lean out into sunshine with beautiful hills and trees and marble churches opposite, and close below, the Arno, gurgling against the embankment of the road."

Leaving the Quisisana's ancient wooden elevator and its wrought-iron cage, we enter a time warp—a bygone world of plush chairs, antimacassars and glass cases full of china cups on display. Nothing in Florence comes close to evoking such vivid memories of the days of Miss Honeychurch and other members of Forster's brave little band of turn-of-the-century travelers.

Immediately to the left is the **Uffizi Gallery (16)**, Italy's most important collection of paintings and one of the world's great galleries.

Just as no visit to Florence is complete without seeing this gallery's many masterpieces, no literary tour of the city is complete without visiting a statue in the Uffizi that has entranced great writers since the 17th century. The statue is the Medici Venus, a 1st-century B.C. Roman copy of an earlier Greek work, and it is still here, in room 18. If English art critic John Ruskin were still around, he would probably suggest you make a direct dash from the entrance, head nonstop to room 18 and remain there for hours esthetically absorbing and otherwise pondering one of the most splendid nudes ever sculpted. On the other hand, you might want to compare your reactions to those of Tobias Smollett, who in 1764 wrote, "It must be want of taste that prevents my feeling that enthusiastic admiration with which others are inspired at sight of this statue." Smollett "could not help thinking that there is no beauty in the features of Venus; and that the attitude is awkward and out of character." Again by contrast, in 1789 Arthur Young wrote in *Travels in France and Italy*, "It is not easy to speak of such divine beauty with any sobriety of language; nor without hyperbole to express one's imagination." His own hyperbole perhaps was to suggest that, after a first viewing, one should "retire to repose on the insipidity of common objects, and return another day, to gaze with fresh admiration." The soul of Russia, Dostoevsky, was entranced by Venus, and even staid New Englander Nathaniel Hawthorne was profoundly affected, writing on one of his pilgrimages that Venus is "as young and fair today as she was three thousand years ago. . . . She is a miracle." The Uffizi is open daily 9–7; Sundays and holidays 9–1; closed Mondays.

Continuing down the Lungarno, at Piazza Cavalleggeri 2, just off the Lungarno delle Grazie, the **Pensione White (17)** was a tidy and organized place catering mainly to English visitors. In the spring of 1910 it was the Florence headquarters of Arnold Bennett, author of *The Old Wives' Tale* and all-round man of letters. His *Florentine Journal* and accompanying sketches provide lively images of 1910 Florence, with wagons and trams drawn by horses "that have to eat while moving," vivid street life and even one of the first (but definitely not the last) Italian garbage strikes. His *Journal* also shows that Bennett led an exemplary intellectual life in Florence, working on his novel ("did 3 full hours on *Clayhanger* before breakfast"), spending evenings at the theater ("went to *Monna Vanna* at the Verdi . . . the worst dramatic performance, without exception, that I have seen anywhere") and hitting all the museums and churches. Aside from these eminently correct activities, his *Journal* also reveals this fastidious and highly cultured man to have been something of a *voyeur*. One entry recounts how he had been strolling for weeks down the Lungarno to the Ponte Vecchio to watch Italian schoolgirls "in their short skirts," concluding that "they are quite *formées*." Although he enjoyed ogling the Italian *ragazze*, Bennett evidently detested the view of his fellow Englishmen, judging one group of tourists "positively a revolting sight."

From the Piazza Cavaleggeri, Corso dei Tintori and then Via Magliabeche lead to the church of **Santa Croce (18)** which, along with its piazza and Renaissance neighborhood, is one of Florence's

Church of Santa Croce

great attractions. Santa Croce dates from the late 13th century and boasts a cavernous and spectacular interior with timbered roof. Its chapels include works by Giotto, Gaddi, della Robbia and other masters. In his *Private Diaries* (1811) Stendhal was enthralled by the Volterrano ceiling frescoes in the Niccolini chapel, to the left of the altar in the north transept, and by Bronzino's "Descent into Limbo," once in the Niccolini chapel but since moved to Santa Croce's museum to the right of the church. Santa Croce is also the Westminster Abbey of Florence, for it is here that Florence buried its greats, including Michelangelo, Machiavelli and Galileo. Lord Byron, greatly moved, wrote in *Childe Harold's Pilgrimage* of the tombs that "in Santa Croce's holy precincts lie."

On November 3, 1838, essayist and author Thomas Babington Macaulay took a less favorable view of Santa Croce. After perusing the latest English newspapers at Vieusseaux's and "greatly admiring a little painting by Raphael, from Ezekiel" at the Pitti Palace (*Ezekiel's Vision* in the Sala di Saturno—room 5), Macaulay went on to find Santa Croce "ugly, mean outside; and not much to admire in the architecture within, but consecrated by the dust of some of the greatest men that ever lived."

On a less serious note, Lucy Honeychurch, the heroine of *Room with a View,* became lost in Santa Croce—trapped there without a Baedeker to tell her which "of all the sepulchral slabs that paved the nave and transepts was the one . . . that had been most praised by Mr. Ruskin." Lucy is fortunately "rescued" by her future husband and his father. Together they "wandered not unpleasantly about Santa Croce, which, though it is like a barn, has harvested many beautiful things inside its walls. There were also beggars to avoid, and guides to dodge round the pillars, and an old lady with her dog, and here and there a priest modestly edging to his Mass through the groups of tourists." Santa Croce is open daily 8–12:30 and 3–6:30.

The Renaissance maze that surrounds Santa Croce has changed little from the days when Michelangelo and Vasari called it home.

Neighborhoods like this in Rome and southern Italy throb with a life that spills out into the streets, but not here. This is a somber district of austere houses with eaves (*sporti*) that extend over the narrow stone streets and the glass lanterns that still light them. Piazza Santa Croce, framed by 14th- and 15th-century houses, is historically one of Florence's great outdoor theaters, having been used over the centuries for civic pageants, the burning of heretics and other municipal sporting events.

It is only fitting that Michelangelo is buried in Santa Croce, for it was his parish church. Three houses belonging to him have been connected over the years and converted into an interesting little museum of his sketches, sculptures and wooden models of his works and drawings. The **Casa Buonarotti (19)**, at Via Ghibellina 70, is open daily 9:30–1:30 except Tuesdays.

Borgo Santa Croce leads from the piazza to the house of Giorgio Vasari. If anyone deserves the title, "Renaissance man," it is surely Vasari, whose home and studio can be found at **Borgo Santa Croce 8 (20)**. Michelangelo undoubtedly knew this house well, for the two were fast friends and mutual admirers. Vasari— artist, master architect, art historian and author—designed the covered "secret" passageway that still connects the Pitti Palace with the Uffizi via the Ponte Vecchio. Although his house has been modernized, traces of the original brickwork are still visible in the courtyard.

Return to the Lungarno and cross the Ponte Vecchio to the part of Florence known as the Oltrarno ("across the Arno").

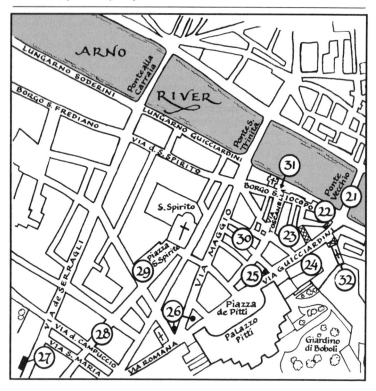

Florence Walk, Part 3: The Oltrarno

Although the "latest" **Ponte Vecchio (21)** dates from 1345, it has been lined with the shops of Florence's famed jewelers and goldsmiths only since 1593, when the stench of the previous meat and fish markets overwhelmed the grand duke of the time. Vasari's corridor, which has connected the Uffizi with the Pitti Palace since 1565, can be seen above the shops on the lefthand side. The corridor is often closed for structural repairs; however, when it is open, tours are conducted every morning except Monday and must be booked in advance at the Uffizi.

The Oltrarno end of the bridge, with its many street vendors selling leather goods and ersatz designer luggage, is just the place to test your negotiating skills. Many of these items are also sold in the stores along **Borgo San Iacopo (22)**, on the right. Further along, the Borgo contains several excellent restaurants.

The house where Niccolo Machiavelli was born in 1469 and died in 1527 stood at **Via Guicciardini 16 (23)** until it was destroyed in World War II. This political genius and statesman was the equivalent of Florence's foreign minister at age 29 and went on to become its ambassador to a number of foreign courts, including Rome, France and Germany, before being exiled. Machiavelli's masterpiece, *The Prince* (the prince in question being the Medici Duke of Urbino, the young son of Lorenzo the Magnificent), written in 1513, is a do-it-yourself guide to power, with advice for the intelligent and wise ruler about attaining and retaining authority. Machiavelli's advice to be feared (but not hated) rather than loved, and armed rather than unarmed and therefore despised, are embedded in our political theory. Unfortunately they did Florence little good, for the Spanish subjugated the city a few years after Machiavelli's death.

Just down the street, at No. 15, is the **Palazzo Guicciar-dini (24)**, a place Machiavelli knew well, for it was the home of his close friend, Francesco Guicciardini. Like Machiavelli a political philosopher and statesman, Guicciardini wrote *History of Italy*, a brilliant account of the tumultuous events of that period. The Guicciardini family still lives in this massive brownstone palace.

In a small apartment at **Piazza di Pitti 21 (25)**, Dostoevsky in 1868 wrote most of *The Idiot*. When not writing he was very much the dedicated tourist, spending much time in the Uffizi. He was particularly smitten by Raffaello's painting of St. John the Baptist, which is still on view in room 18.

At the other end of the Piazza di Pitti, at Piazza San Felice 8, stands the 15th-century **Casa Guidi (26)**, modest and not

particularly distinguished. But in the last century, as the home of
Robert and Elizabeth Barrett Browning, Casa Guidi was one of the
most famous literary addresses in Europe.

The newly (and secretly) wed Brownings arrived in Florence in
April 1847, taking up temporary lodgings on the other side of the
Arno at Via delle Belle Donne 6, just off Piazza Santa Maria
Novella. Two months later, during a sizzling Florentine summer,
Elizabeth wrote,

> Robert went out to find cool rooms, to make the best of our position,
> and now we are settled magnificently in this Palazzo Guidi [in] a suite
> of spacious rooms opening on a little terrace and furnished elegantly
> . . . but cool and in a delightful situation six paces from the Piazza di
> Pitti and with right of daily admission to the Boboli Gardens. . . .
> Isn't this prosperous?

The Brownings were to establish their "headquarters" at Casa
Guidi for fourteen years, until Elizabeth died here in June 1861.
Casa Guidi was very dear to the Brownings and, for the invalid
Elizabeth, was "my chimney corner." It was also the scene of the
Brownings' fabled marital bliss and the birth of their son Pen in
1849.

The Brownings' life at Casa Guidi centered around intellectual
conversations, carefully selected visitors, writing and the pampered
upbringing of their only child. Here they wrote *Christmas Eve and
Easter Day, Aurora Leigh,* and, of course, *Old Pictures in Florence.*
On the narrow balcony Robert composed *The Ring and the Book.*
Although scores of European and American writers and intellec-
tuals, including novelists Harriet Beecher Stowe and Anthony
Trollope, Tennyson, the Hawthornes, and James Russell Lowell
(who sublet the apartment from the Brownings in the fall of 1851),
crossed the threshold of Casa Guidi, the Brownings idyllic life here
was largely self-contained.

The Brownings' salon was not, however, exclusively literary or
intellectual; both Robert and Elizabeth were strong political
supporters of the *risorgimento,* the Italian independence movement

demanding freedom from Austria, and they knew many of its leaders—Garibaldi, Mazzini and Cavour. Their enthusiasm for Italian independence is reflected in Robert's lines from *Old Pictures in Florence* about "the new tricolor that flaps in the sky" and Elizabeth's *Casa Guidi Windows* with its ode to "beautiful liberty."

After Elizabeth's death Robert returned frequently to Italy, but never to Florence, with its bittersweet memories. Elizabeth is buried in a tomb designed by Robert in Florence's Protestant Cemetery, in Piazza Donatello, just outside the city center (open 9–12 and 3–5). Robert died in Venice in 1889 and lies in

The Ponte Vecchio

Westminster Abbey. Their apartment is now owned by the
Browning Institute and can be visited daily from 10–12 and 3–6,
except Mondays.

After leaving Casa Guidi follow Via Romana to Via del
Campuccio, which leads to Via de Serragli.

Nathaniel Hawthorne, accompanied by his wife and their three
children, left Rome for Florence in May 1858. The author's son,
writing much later, thought his father's stay in Florence had been
"the happiest period in Hawthorne's life."

The Hawthornes settled quickly into the ground floor of the
sprawling, 17-room **Casa Bella (27)**, located at Via de' Serragli
132. In keeping with its highly unoriginal name, Casa Bella was
then fresh and bright looking, with large, comfortable rooms, a
broad terrace and access to the adjacent Torrigiani Gardens. Most
importantly for a writer, Hawthorne noted that he had "the
pleasantest room for my study and . . . I can overflow into the
summer-house or an arbor and sit there dreaming of a story." The
rent for this spacious furnished apartment was all of $50 per
month, causing Hawthorne to exclaim that Florence was "a
paradise of cheapness."

At Casa Bella Hawthorne continued work begun in Rome on
The Marble Faun. Like their friends the Brownings, the
Hawthornes were driven out of Florence by the summer heat.
Their refuge was the equally agreeable Villa Montauto, just out of
town on the Via San Carlo in Bellosguardo, which became the
model for the villa in *The Marble Faun.* A plaque on Casa Bella
marks Hawthorne's stay.

Return on Via de Serragli to Via Santa Maria, an ageless street
of artisan workshops and drying laundry, after which a left turn on
Via delle Caldaie (28), named for the cauldrons of the wool-dyers
that once labored here, leads past elegant palaces with trompe
l'oeil paintings on their walls. As you prowl the homes and shops
of this fascinating neighborhood, you may notice that many faces
seem vaguely familiar. These are precisely the classic Florentine

faces that gaze down from medieval and Renaissance paintings in the Uffizi, Pitti Palace and other museums all over the world.

When Via delle Caldaie reaches the charming **Piazza Santo Spirito (29)** and its Brunelleschi church, we enter the Florence of Giovanni Boccaccio, who spent his youth in the labyrinth of medieval streets inside the triangle formed by the Ponte Vecchio, the church of Santo Spirito and the Pitti Palace.

Boccaccio's towering literary work is of course *The Decameron*, a 14th-century masterpiece of lively, well-told and often bawdy stories. It was the first piece of modern Italian prose and has been a model for short-story collections of all kinds ever since, including another literary milestone, Chaucer's *Canterbury Tales.* Set in the hills near Florence in 1348, the terrible Year of the Black Death, *The Decameron* (a word invented by Boccaccio based on the Greek words for "10" and "day") contains 100 tales told in 10 days by 10 young fugitives from the plague who evidently believed that "the surest medicine for so much evil was to drink heavily and enjoy things [and go] around singing and making merry and satisfying every appetite they could, laughing and ridiculing whatever might happen."

The literary outcome of Boccaccio's imaginative and painless remedy for a pandemic that killed thousands did not sit well with many. Mr. T. Adolphus Trollope, a 19th-century English writer resident in Florence, sniffed "[A] few of the stories are such as no decent woman would like to confess that she had read, and no man of ordinary refined taste would care to read."

To explore Boccaccio's world, wander along the Via Maggio with its antique shops and palaces of the 14th–16th centuries, turn right onto the **Via dei Velluti (30)** and left onto **Via Toscanella (31)**. A right turn at the end of Via Toscanella onto Via San Iacopo leads onto Via Guicciardini; a few steps to the right is Boccaccio's parish church, **Santa Felicita (32)**. The facade of this quiet oasis, which dates back to the first days of Christianity, is by Vasari. Inside are splendid works by Pontormo.

San Marco

Venice

"VENICE IS LIKE eating an entire box of chocolate liqueurs at one go," wrote Truman Capote. Even jaded travelers find this city a magical, almost supernatural experience. No matter how or how often you have traveled to this unique and beautiful city, every visit brings the thrill and surprise of discovering what Howells called its "peerless strangeness." Arriving by auto at the mega-garages of Piazzale Roma or by train at Santa Lucia station, you are immediately confronted by the bustling boat traffic of the Grand Canal—a reminder of American humorist Robert Benchley's cable, "Streets full of water. Please advise." But the most dramatic arrival of all is from the airport, a boast few other cities can make. Anticipation builds as your water taxi passes a scattering of low islands, then comes San Michele, the cemetery island where American poet Ezra Pound is buried, and finally Venice appears on the horizon, Longfellow's "white swan of cities," rising like an apparition from the lagoon. Wondrous details begin to appear— church domes and bell towers, mighty brick and marble palaces, the maze of tiny canals and streets that filter, like capillaries, back into the heart of this ageless and secret place. Then, at last, Venice's splendid front door, the magnificent Doge's Palace and the ancient columns of the Piazzetta di San Marco.

Even the briefest of visits reveals why this spectacularly beautiful and romantic city has attracted artists, composers and writers from the very dawn of modern travel. Many others, however, more prosaically thought of Venice not as one of the West's great treasures, but as the hub of a great trading empire that was once, as Baedeker tells us, "the focus of the commerce of Europe." Years after the explorations of native son Marco Polo, Venetian ships and galleys crisscrossed the Mediterranean, traded with the Orient and even called regularly at the Channel ports, thereby spreading the city's fame and influence to 16th-century England. So great was Venice's reputation for wealth, intrigue and power that William Shakespeare was moved to write two plays, *Othello* and *The Merchant of Venice,* about life, death and betrayal in a fabled city he had never seen.

The Grand Canal

In the centuries that followed, Venice became one of Europe's great literary destinations, casting an irresistible spell over 19th-century romantics of all nations. But, for inexplicable reasons, it was Anglo-Saxons such as Ruskin, James and Howells, rather than Italian or continental writers, who best captured the spirit and splendor of the city. Venice, in fact, has never truly become Italian, European or even of this century; of all the world's settlements it stands alone and unmatchable, as James Morris observed in his 1960 classic *Venice,* because of "the brilliance and strangeness of her history, the wide melancholy lagoon that surrounds her, the convoluted sea splendor that keeps her, to this day, unique among the cities."

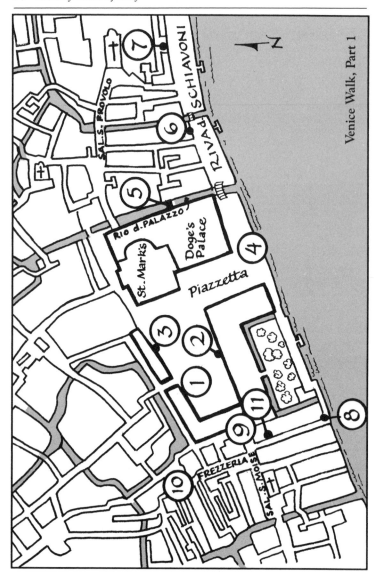

Venice Walk, Part 1

Venice Walk, Part 1: Around the Piazza San Marco

Our amphibious tour of literary Venice begins in St. Mark's Square, or **Piazza San Marco (1)**, which since the 9th century has been the city's heart and soul as well as a magnificent stage for the vivid pageant of Venetian life. For 1000 years the piazza has captivated writers, artists and ordinary visitors; even Venice's sworn enemy Napoleon, who put an end to the Venetian Republic in 1797, called it "the finest drawing room in Europe." Goethe thought it could be compared only to itself. Although at the height of the tourist season in high summer, San Marco can be crowded, noisy and very commercial (perhaps prompting Henry James's remark, "Though there are some disagreeable things in Venice there is nothing so disagreeable as the visitors"), most of us would still agree with 17th-century traveler Thomas Coryate that "truely such is the stupendious . . . glory of it, that at my first entrance thereof it did even amaze or rather ravish my senses."

San Marco is especially ravishing if you first glimpse it at dusk on a soft spring evening, at the precise moment when the lights that ring the piazza come on while a string orchestra plays at one of the outdoor cafes. Or you might arrive during one of the heavy fogs of autumn that turn Venice into a ghostly city of immense mystery and romance, where bells ring out from unseen churches, palaces on the Grand Canal become shrouded and the cathedral becomes a shadowy form crouching in the mist at the end of the square. But late in the evening, when the piazza empties, with a little imagination you might be able to visualize some of the literary ghosts who have loved and written about this great square.

On the south side at **Florian's (2)**, Italy's oldest *caffe*, Henry James had his usual early breakfast, Baedeker at the ready. James once described the pleasures of "taking one's coffee at Florian's" in *The Aspern Papers*, whose narrator spends his evenings here,

> eating ices, listening to music, talking with acquaintances: the traveller will remember how the immense cluster of tables and little chairs stretches like a promontory into the smooth lake of the Piazza.

It still does. At a nearby table we might spot French novelist Marcel Proust, who also spent hours at Florian's, eating ices and watching the pigeons in "a vast and splendid campo . . . flanked with charming palaces silvery in the moonlight."

Both of these ghosts would recognize today's Florian's which, with its small rooms covered with mirrors and glass-paned prints, creaky parquet floors and marble tables, literally reeks of the last century.

Across the Piazza, at that other great *caffe*, **Quadri (3)**, we might find Charles Dickens, bowled over by his first impressions of this glorious square: "The wildest visions of the Arabian Nights are nothing to the Piazza of Saint Mark." In *Pictures from Italy* Dickens describes

> a place of such surpassing beauty, and such grandeur, that all the rest was poor and faded, in comparison with its absorbing loveliness. . . . An oblong square of lofty houses of the whitest stone, surrounded by a light and beautiful arcade, formed part of this enchanted scene; and here and there, gay masts for flags rose.

We might also see a plump and extravagantly dressed Englishman leave one of the piazza's crowded cafes and hobble away toward his lodgings on the Frezzeria. That would be Lord Byron, possibly composing some verses for *Childe Harold's Pilgrimage* ("Before St. Mark still glow his steeds of brass / their gilded collars glittering in the sun"), but much more likely thinking of an imminent rendezvous with the landlord's wife, Marianna Segati, in his rooms over a draper's shop that bore, appropriately enough, the sign of "the horn."

Another ghostly figure might be a lanky, elegant Englishman, notebook in hand, ready to sketch the church of San Marco. John Ruskin, then in the second year of a six-year marriage that was never consummated, at least knew Venice intimately and dubbed the cathedral "a confusion of delight." However, Ruskin, ever the superesthete, mourned that the Venetians, just like the Romans and other disrespectful Italians, paid little attention to this "treasure heap" in their midst: "Round the whole square in front of the church there is almost a continuous line of cafes, where the idle Venetians of the middle class lounge, and read empty journals." Ruskin would be dismayed to learn that the piazza is still the caloric hub of Venice, with hundreds of tourist-oriented restaurants and *pizzerie* in the surrounding area.

Much later, American novelist and critic Mary McCarthy took quite a different view of the cathedral, saying it was "not beautiful," the mosaics are "generally admitted to be extremely ugly," and as for the rest, "It is better not to look too closely." Take your choice.

And finally, our last specter is that of Abraham Lincoln's representative in Venice, American Consul William Dean Howells. The essayist, editor and future author of *The Rise of Silas Lapham* wrote in 1862 of peering through a heavy snowfall for "a faint glimpse of the golden winged angel on the bell-tower of St. Mark's" and of the gauzy beauty of the cathedral and its piazza in the snow ("What summer-delight of other lands could match the beauty of the first Venetian snowfall which I saw?"). Howells, like many diplomats, was underworked at his post and spent many hours at Florian's, which in those days was the only *caffe* frequented by both the Venetians and their Austrian occupiers; others were strictly self-segregated along national lines.

After passing the Doge's Palace and the two 12th-century columns in the piazzetta you will be on the **Riva degli Schiavoni (4)**, which James compared to the promenade deck for the salon of the piazza. A left turn on the Riva, which is now an area of open-air stands and quai-side restaurants, leads to the Bridge of Sighs.

The **Bridge of Sighs (5)**, which crosses the Rio di Palazzo just after you pass the Doge's Palace, owes much of its fame to Lord Byron, whose *Childe Harold's Pilgrimage* ("I stood in Venice on the Bridge of Sighs; / A Palace and a prison on each hand") immortalized forever this attractive little bridge. Less charitably,

The Bridge of Sighs

Howells called the bridge a "pathetic swindle," while Ruskin deemed it "a work of no merit . . . owing the interest it possesses chiefly to its pretty name and to the ignorant sentimentalism of Byron."

Incidentally, the canal steps just under the bridge you are standing on were the scene for intense (and unwanted) local color for young Henry Wadsworth Longfellow, who, in 1828, was blissfully sketching the Bridge of Sighs when "a wench of a chambermaid emptied a pitcher of water from a window of the palace directly upon my head. I came very near slipping into the canal." *Attenzione!*

The **Hotel Danieli (6)**, at Riva degli Schiavoni 4196, is one of Italy's most distinguished hotels and a leading literary landmark. In the 15th century the Danieli was the Palazzo Dandolo, which was converted into a hotel in 1822 by one Joseph dal Niel, who combined his name with that of the previous owner to make Danieli. The hotel has always been a mecca for visiting writers, including Ruskin, a frequent visitor, who wrote much of *The Stones of Venice* here, Marcel Proust, and Charles Dickens, who came here in 1844 and again in 1853.

Dickens wrote to a friend that his apartment at the Danieli was at the corner of the house,

> and there is a narrow street of water running round the side . . . with three arched windows . . . looking down upon the Grand Canal, and away, beyond, to where the sun went down tonight in a blaze.

Dickens was fascinated by the lively dockside scene below, including "great ships lying at hand in stately indolence" and "islands, crowned with gorgeous domes and turrets . . . where golden crosses glittered in the light, atop of wondrous churches springing from the sea!"

Ruskin has always been controversial. Henry James, who seemed to admire Ruskin's thoughts on Venice, nevertheless mocked and attacked his super-refined descriptions of Florence. Baedeker advised his many faithful that "the intelligent traveler will temper Mr. Ruskin's extreme and sometimes extraordinary statements with his own discretion." But, despite Ruskin's precious writing, wildly opinionated views on art and obviously bizarre marital life, his *Stones of Venice* remains one of the great guides for visitors to the lagoon; after almost 150 years it is still considered among the definitive works on the art and architecture of Venice. Much of this magisterial work was written in room 32 of the Danieli between 1849 and 1850. In that year, Effie Ruskin enjoyed a lively social life with the Austrian nobility and officials who then occupied Venice while her husband sketched, pondered and wrote. Although *Stones of Venice* originally appeared in three dense volumes, a condensed version is still available.

Room 10 of the Danieli was the scene of one of literature's most celebrated tiffs. It was to this corner suite in 1833 that French novelist George Sand and poet Alfred de Musset came in search of romantic love, 19th-century style. Unfortunately Musset was more interested in carousing than in George. When he fell seriously ill at the Danieli, she embarked on an affair with his physician.

Marcel Proust, another noted Danieli guest, was so taken with Venice during his first visit in May 1900 that he exclaimed that his dream had become his address. The impact of Venice was still vivid twenty-five years later when in *Remembrance of Things Past* he wrote, "After dinner I went out by myself, into the heart of the enchanted city where I found myself wandering in strange regions like a character in *The Arabian Nights*. It was very seldom that I did not, in the course of my wanderings, hit upon some strange and spacious piazza of which no guidebook, no tourist had ever told me."

Walk down to **Riva degli Schiavoni 4161 (7)**, where Henry James rented a fourth-floor apartment on his 1881 visit. Venice became a lifelong passion for James, one that endured even though he eventually soured on his other Italian passions, Rome and Florence, which became "vulgarized." On James's farewell visit a quarter century later, he found Venice "never . . . more lovable."

James's rooms on the Riva were evidently far from luxurious. He said they were, in fact, "dirty apartments with a lovely view." The spectacular panorama from James's fourth-floor windows held a continual fascination for him, from the animated street and nautical life on the Riva below to the view across the lagoon.

> Straight across, before my windows, rose the great pink mass of San Giorgio Maggiore, which has for a Palladian church a success beyond all reason, . . . a kind of suffusion of rosiness.

Despite these strong distractions and the "fruitless fidget of composition," James finished *The Portrait of a Lady* here on Riva degli Schiavioni.

The building where James stayed is still a *pensione,* now called the Wildner. To get his old room, ask for No. 47.

An about-face and a walk down the Riva to its very end brings us to the San Marco *vaporetto* (water bus) stop, where we turn right on the Calle Vallaresso and enter **Harry's Bar (8)**.

Aside from being the world's best-known bar, Harry's is one of the few literary shrines that offer pilgrims exceptional martinis and one of the best kitchens in Italy. This charming and cozy restaurant has long been a magnet for visiting celebrities, including novelist Ernest Hemingway, who used Harry's as his personal club when he was in town. Hemingway spent many convivial hours at the small bar, often with his good friend, owner Arrigo Cipriani. Hemingway later immortalized Harry's in *Across the River and into the Trees* as the place where the book's hero, Colonel Cantwell, consumes many of Cipriani's famed martinis and where, on one occasion, Hemingway takes a vicious literary swing at his fellow American novelist, Sinclair Lewis, "the man at the third table [who had] a strange face, . . . as pockmarked and as blemished as the mountains of the moon."

Hemingway and his wife Mary also stayed at Cipriani's *Locanda* on the island of Torcello during a November 1948 visit, when, according to English novelist Anthony Burgess, "Venice became his new mistress."

A very different writer, the American Truman Capote, was also a Harry's devotee from his first stay in July 1948, during that happy postwar era of the almighty dollar when cocktails cost only twenty-five cents and thick steaks only a bit more. On a 1956 visit, when he was staying at art patron Peggy Guggenheim's *palazzo* across the Grand Canal and working on *The Muses Are Heard,* Capote again made Harry's his dining room and clubhouse.

At the other end of Calle Vallaresso, **Salizzada San Moise (9)** has many luxury stores bearing the names of major fashion houses, while straight ahead is Byron's **Frezzeria (10)**, then as now a street of shops and stores. On the way, the **Hotel Luna (11)**, on the righthand side of Calle Vallaresso, was Stendhal's home during his 1828 visit.

Venice "Walk," Part 2: The Grand Canal

The daily pageant of the Grand Canal and an exploration of this dazzling boulevard by gondola are, even as we approach the 21st century, high on almost anyone's list of unforgettable travel experiences. Karl Baedeker noted, "At every turn the winding canal reveals new beauties," but he characteristically went on to warn travelers about "the importunities of the boatmen." Still good advice. But, despite the surrealism of boats that deliver appliances, haul garbage, carry wedding parties and perform other tasks we usually associate with wheels and not hulls, it is the gondolier who for centuries has been the symbol of Venice and its romance. The 19th-century English poet Arthur Henry Clough wrote:

> How light we move, how swiftly, ah
> Were life but as the gondola.

Perhaps the best description of the delights of gondola travel is Proust's narrative in *Remembrance of Things Past*:

> We returned up the Grand Canal in our gondola. We watched the double line of palaces . . . reflect the light and angle of the sun upon their rosy surfaces, . . . seeming not so much private habitations and historic buildings as a chain of marble cliffs at the foot of which people go out in the evening in a boat to watch the sunset . . . in this Venice where the simplest social coming and going assumed at the same time the form and the charm of a visit to a museum and a trip to the sea.

At the **San Marco** *vaporetto* stop **(12)**, take a line 1,2 or 4 water bus marked Ferrovia.

On the right the splendidly Gothic **Palazzo Giustinian (13)**, now the headquarters for the famed *Biennale* art and film festivals but earlier the Hotel Europa, was home in 1869 to Mark Twain. Even this crusty "innocent abroad" fell victim to the charms of Venice; although his evening arrival was marred by a singing *gondoliere* ("a mangy, barefooted guttersnipe"), Twain was forced to admit that:

> Under the mellow moonlight the Venice of poetry and romance stood
> revealed. Right from the water's edge rose long lines of stately marble.
> . . . There was life and motion everywhere and yet everywhere there
> was a hush, a stealthy sort of stillness, that was suggestive of secret
> enterprises of bravoes and of lovers.

Next door, Russian playwright and short storyteller Anton
Chekhov stayed in the now much-reconstructed **Hotel Bauer-
Grunwald (14)** in March 1891 and wrote to his brother,

> All I can say is never in my life have I seen a city more remarkable
> than Venice. Such fascination, such glitter, such exuberance! . . .
> And the evenings! Good Lord in Heaven! I could die from the
> novelty of it all.

Also on the right, the **Hotel Gritti (15)**, located in the 15th-
century Palazzo Pisani, was Hemingway's Venetian command post
during his two visits. Hemingway wrote in 1949 that the Gritti was
(it very likely still is) "probably the best hotel . . . in a city of great
hotels." As readers of *Across the River and into the Trees* will recall,
the doomed Colonel Cantwell and his teenage love, Renata, have
their final trysts at the Gritti and from here take their portentous
gondola rides in the "cold wind."

During his 1949 visit Hemingway stayed in suite 115/116 but
spent considerable time at "the bar just across from the lobby," a
massive, white stone affair with splendid inlays of yellow and green
marble. The then-manager recalled that the great man often
started his day with three bottles of wine, followed by a parade of
spirits that lasted well into the evening. On his return to Venice
and the Gritti in 1954, Hemingway was recuperating from serious
and painful injuries suffered in an African plane crash; his
weakened state did not, however, keep him from a friendly and
animated game of night baseball (the first ever in Palazzo Pisani),
which resulted in a smashed lobby window.

On the right, just before the Accademia bridge, is the
sumptuous **Palazzo Barbaro (16)** and its wealthy Bostonian owners,
Daniel and Ariana Curtis. Here in the elegant top-floor apartment

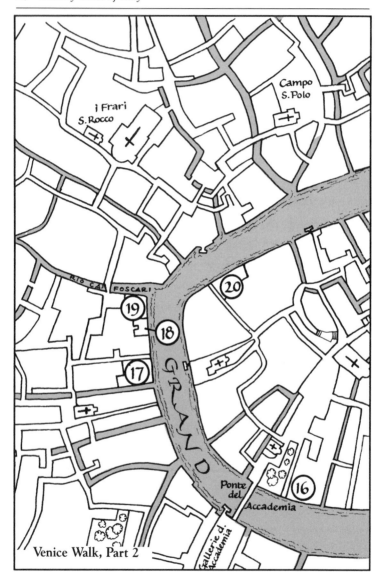

Venice Walk, Part 2

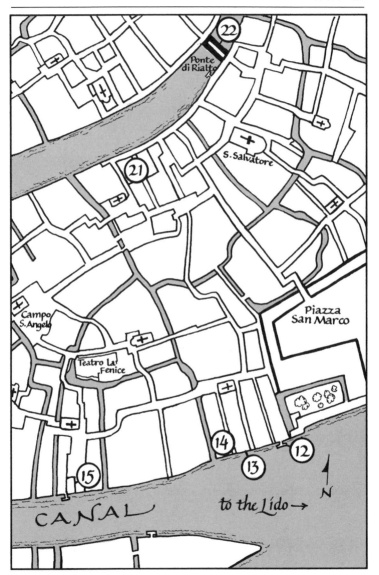

Ponte
di Rialto

S. Salvatore

Campo
S. Angelo

Teatro La
Fenice

Piazza
San Marco

CANAL

to the Lido →

N

James worked on *The Aspern Papers,* which is set in Venice but based on an anecdote about Byron's papers that actually occurred in Florence. During a stay in 1889 he gathered atmosphere for the final chapters of *The Wings of the Dove,* which, in repayment to the Curtises, took place in their palazzo.

Soon after passing under the bridge, watch for an imposing building on the left with arched windows and pillared balconies. This is the **Palazzo Rezzonico (17)**, bought in 1887 by Robert Browning's son Pen, who had the foresight to marry an American heiress. It was on a visit to the Rezzonico, which the poet called "a corner for my old age," that Robert caught cold and died. A plaque on the side canal marks the occasion and records two lines from his poem, "De Gustibus":

> Open my heart and you will see
> Graved inside of it, Italy.

Browning's small room, which has been left as it was, is frequently closed. The splendid rooms of the Rezzonico also contain the Museum of 18th-Century Venetian Art, which includes a number of fine works by Tiepolo and Longhi. The museum is open from 10–4 (9:30–12:30 Sundays and holidays) but closed on Fridays. As with all Venetian museums, it is best to check the hours first.

Two palaces away from the Rezzonico, the 15th-century **Palazzo Giustinian (18)** was, in 1864–65, the home and office of William Dean Howells, who had been granted the sinecure of American Consul by President Lincoln as compensation for a highly effective campaign biography. The Howells' six-room apartment, for which the young consul paid $1 per day, was on the first floor (by European reckoning) on the righthand end of the building. From its balconied windows, which he called "the finest position on the Grand Canal," Howells watched the nonstop pageant of canal traffic, from the gondolas bearing tourists of all nations to the barges and boats that hauled freight and sold fuel, fish and vegetables.

At Palazzo Giustinian Howells worked on *Venetian Life,* an immensely captivating and incisive memoir that captures in rich detail Venetian life in the final days of Austrian rule. Although Howells was enthralled by that long-ago snowfall in Piazza San Marco, he also described the downside of the Venetian winter, with its glooms, rigors and icy winds ("all the floors are death-cold in winter. People sit with their feet upon cushions and their bodies muffled in furs and wadded gowns. . . . Indeed the sun is recognized by Venetians as the only legitimate source of heat").

By contrast, the long Venetian summers were much more agreeable for the American Consul, for he was able to plunge into the Grand Canal from the doorway under his windows for his regular morning swim. Although swimming in the canal's polluted

Market on the Rialto

waters today would border on insanity, conditions in 1865 must have been very different:

> When the tide comes in fresh and strong from the sea the water in the Grand Canal is pure and refreshing; and at these times it is a singular pleasure to leap from one's door-step into the swift current, and spend a half-hour, very informally, among one's neighbors there.

Next to Howell's palazzo, where Rio Foscari enters the Grand Canal, stands **Ca' Foscari (19)**, the palace that Ruskin called the "noblest example in Venice of the 15th Century Gothic."

Just around the bend after Ca' Foscari, on the righthand side, are the **Mocenigo palaces (20)**, easily identified by their blue and white striped poles. The Mocenigo palaces were built separately by one of Venice's great families but years ago were covered by a unifying facade. From 1816 to 1819 Lord Byron lived in the center palazzo, the one with the plaque, leading a fantastic and gaudy lifestyle that would have astounded even the Mocenigo doges.

Byron's years in Palazzo Mocenigo included bursts of great creativity. It was here that he began work on his masterpiece, *Don Juan*, but it was also a time of what biographer Andre Maurois called "extreme debauchery." Byron took to the palazzo an extraordinary menage that included "caged wild animals and uncaged mistresses" plus fourteen servants, a wolf, two monkeys, a fox and two mastiffs. Life at Mocenigo also included a parade of lovers, one of whom, in a fit of jealous rage at finding Byron already occupied with a rival, jumped into the canal from the front steps while brandishing a table knife.

Like Howells, Byron was an enthusiastic canal swimmer and, like the legendary callgirl in Venice, sometimes swam to and from romantic appointments. According to one account, Byron was once seen "leaving a party, to throw himself into the Canal fully dressed . . . swimming with one hand, and in the other holding a lantern to warn approaching gondoliers."

On the right, just before the Rialto water-taxi stop, the twin

Palazzi Farsetti-Loredan (21) are wonderful examples of Veneto-Byzantine architecture of the 12th and 13th centuries. In fact Ruskin thought the white stone Palazzo Loredan nearest the bridge, "the most beautiful palace in the whole extent of the Grand Canal." It is now Venice's City Hall. Its smaller neighbor, Palazzo Farsetti, was rented by James Fenimore Cooper during an 1838 visit. Far from his pathfinders and deerslayers, Cooper soon found that "although Venice was attractive at first, in the absence of acquaintances it became monotonous and wearying. I do not recollect ever to have been so soon tired of a residence in a capital." He also complained of the city's quiet and stillness, nowadays thought to be a boon beyond measure, especially by those arriving in Venice from the average high-decibel Italian town.

Although there is a house on the Campo del Carmine that guides will swear belonged to Othello, nothing conjures up the Venice of William Shakespeare more than the **Rialto (22)**. When Shylock asked, "What news on the Rialto?" he was asking for the latest from Venice's vibrant commercial world, for the area around the famed bridge was then the trade and financial heart of one of the world's first economic superpowers. Shylock's words, "The trade and profit of this State consisteth of all nations," were no exaggeration.

On the spot where today's Venetians gather on the Rialto to buy fruits and vegetables at the large food halls (at the end of the bridge) along the Ruga degli Orefici (Street of the Goldsmiths), mighty ships once unloaded fabulous cargoes of silks and spices from the East. Here, too, were the great Venetian banks, which invested in these great voyages, pioneered modern banking and extended credits to Shylock and the other merchants of Venice.

Most experts agree that Shakespeare never saw Venice but took the idea for *The Merchant of Venice* from *Il Pecorone,* an Italian tale of the 1550s, just as he borrowed *Othello* from another Italian story of the time.

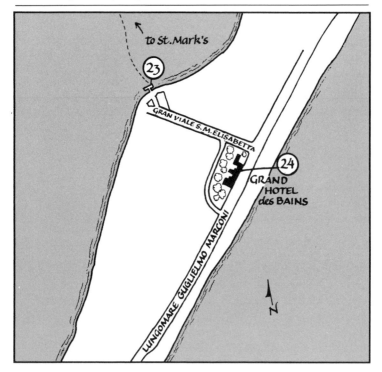

Venice Walk, Part 3: The Lido

Since no literary description of Venice would be complete without *Death in Venice,* from the Rialto take water-bus line 1, 2 or 4 (marked Lido) in the opposite direction. At the **Lido (23)** stop, walk straight ahead to the oceanfront Lungomare Marconi and the **Grand Hotel des Bains (24)**.

At the turn of the century, German novelist Thomas Mann took his family to the sprawling "des Bains" for a vacation among the wealthy international crowd that this luxurious and graceful old hotel still attracts. *Death in Venice* is directly drawn from this experience, which began in the hotel's elegant dining room, where

Mann spotted Tadzio, the beautiful 13-year-old that inspired his masterpiece. Although the protagonist, Aschenbach, is largely modeled on the composer Gustav Mahler, Mann also gave him a number of his own features and personal habits. As for the story itself, Mann wrote,

Nothing is invented in *Death in Venice.* The "pilgrim" at the North Cemetery, the dreary Pola boat, the gray-haired rake, the sinister gondolier, Tadzio and his family, the journey interrupted by a mistake about the luggage, the cholera, the upright clerk at the travel bureau . . . they were all there.

The Lido was also a favorite spot for Lord Byron who, while living in the Mocenigo Palaces, regularly came here for "a gallop of some miles daily along the strip of beach which reaches to Malamocco."

He saw it again: that stupendous waterfront, that astonishing composition of fantastic edifices that the Serenissima presented to the reverent gaze of the navigators that approached it. The airy magnificence of the Doge's Palace and the Bridge of Sighs, the columns on the quay with the Lion and the Saint . . . it was said that arriving in Venice by land was like entering a palazzo through the service entrance and that only by ship, from the open sea, as he had done this time, should one come to the world's most unbelievable city.

– Thomas Mann
Death in Venice

Buon Appetito!

Any stroll through Italian cities, with their enticing food displays, seductive menus in restaurant windows, and pervasive aromas of freshly baked bread and ground *espresso* is sure to stimulate strong interest in sustenance. Since you are in Italy, an authentic culinary superpower, you'll find no lack of possibilities.

The basic unit of refreshment in Italy is the local bar, or *caffe,* where the favored beverage is *espresso* in all its infinite variations, including *espresso doppio* or double, guaranteed to provide a jump start to the day, *espresso macchiato,* with a dash of cold milk, and the ubiquitous *cappuccino,* which only tourists drink after mid-morning. If you prefer your coffee in a glass, ask for it *in vetro;* if you want it decaffeinated, ask for *decaffeinato.*

Bars also provide inexpensive alternatives to hotel breakfasts, which tend to be costly. Start your walk by asking the barman for a *spremuta di arancia* (freshly squeezed orange juice), a *cornetto* (crescent shaped roll), and a *cappuccino scuro,* made with double espresso. Note: in Italian bars the first stop is the cashier, who collects payment after hearing your order and gives you a register receipt, which you give the barman along with your request. A tip of 100-300 lire is usual, depending on the size of your order and the elegance of the bar.

Italian bars also offer a variety of snacks, such as a grilled ham and cheese sandwich, or *toast,* and a more elaborate sandwich with a variety of fillings called a *tramezzino.* In hot weather take a table in the shade and ask for a *granita di caffe con panna,* a wonderful combination of espresso and whipped cream over shaved ice. Keep in mind that table service is much more costly than standing up; to avoid embarrassment never try to take your order away from the bar to an outside table.

For more serious dining, a vast array of establishments stand ready to help; the choice will depend on the level of your starvation and your budget. At the less expensive end of the scale, you could visit a **tavola calda,** a bar serving hot dishes and cold salads, a **pizzeria** serving pizza by the slice to take away, or a **rosticceria,** which features roast chicken. Further upscale is the **trattoria,** which is less pretentious and usually cheaper than the **ristorante,** a full-fledged restaurant.

Although dining habits are changing, lunch in the **trattorie** and **ristoranti** is still a major meal for most Italians and is served from around 12:30 to about 2:00 P.M.; Italians usually gather for dinner between 8:00 and 9:00. Remember that in Italy pasta precedes the entree; ordering it as a main course will not endear you to restaurant owners, whose livelihood depends on serving a first course that is followed by meat or fish.

Further Reading

Amfitheatrof, Erik. *The Enchanted Ground; Americans in Italy 1760-1980*. Boston: Little, Brown, 1980.

Baker, Paul Raymond. *The Fortunate Pilgrims, Americans in Italy 1800-1860*. Cambridge: Harvard University Press, 1964.

Brooks, Van Wyck. *The Dream of Arcadia: American Writers and Artists in Italy, 1760-1915*. New York: E.P. Dutton & Co., 1958.

Edel, Leon. *Henry James, A Life*. New York: Harper & Row, 1985.

Hawthorne, Nathaniel. *The French and Italian Notebooks*, ed. by Thomas Woodson. Columbus: Ohio State University, 1980.

Hibbert, Christopher. *The Grand Tour*. London: Weidenfeld and Nicholson, 1969.

Howells, William Dean. *Venetian Life*. Marlboro, VT: Marlboro Press, 1989.

James, Henry. *Italian Hours*. New York: Ecco Press, 1987.

McCarthy, Mary. *The Stones of Florence* and *Venice Observed*. New York: Penguin, 1985.

Vidal, Gore. *Vidal in Venice*. New York: Summit Books, 1985.

To experience the Italy of Henry James, Miss Honeychurch and other 19th-century travelers, there is nothing like using the guidebooks they used. Baedeker's original guides from that era are available in many used book stores at reasonable cost. For Rome, try Baedeker's *Central Italy* for 1890, while for Florence and Venice the 1889 edition of *Northern Italy* is best. There is also an abbreviated guide covering all three cities, *Italy from the Alps to Naples*, which first appeared in 1909.

Index